CAPTAIN SULLY'S RIVER LANDING

The Hudson Hero of Flight 1549

BY STEVEN OTFINOSKI

Consultant:
Richard Bell, PhD
Associate Professor of History
University of Maryland, College Park

CAPSTONE PRESS
a capstone imprint

Tangled History is published by Capstone Press,
1710 Roe Crest Drive, North Mankato, Minnesota 56003
www.mycapstone.com

Library of Congress Cataloging-in-Publication Data
Names: Otfinoski, Steven, author. Title: Captain Sully's River landing : the Hudson
hero of flight 1549 / by Steven Otfinoski.
Description: North Mankato, Minnesota : Capstone Press, [2019] | Series: Tangled
history | Audience: Age 8-14.
Identifiers: LCCN 2018046549| ISBN 9781543541953 (hardcover) | ISBN 9781543541991
(pbk.) | ISBN 9781543542035 (ebook pdf)
Subjects: LCSH: US Airways Flight 1549 Crash Landing, Hudson River, N.Y. and
N.J., 2009—Juvenile literature. | Airplane crash survival—Juvenile literature.
| Airplanes—Ditching—Hudson River (N.Y. and N.J.)—Juvenile literature. |
Sullenberger, Chesley, 1951—Juvenile literature.
Classification: LCC TL553.525.H83 O44 2019 | DDC 363.12/4097471—dc23
LC record available at https://lccn.loc.gov/2018046549

Editorial Credits
Nick Healy, editor; Tracy McCabe, designer; Svetlana Zhurkin, media researcher;
Laura Manthe, production specialist

Photo Credits
AP Photo: Brad Coville, File/Bebeto Matthews, cover, 94, Greg Lam Pak Ng, 46, Trela
Media, 37; Dreamstime: Giovanni Gagliardi, 34; Getty Images: Bloomberg/Daniel Acker,
8, Daniel Barry, 70, 90, Mark Wilson, 80, NY Daily News Archive/John Roca, 88, NY Daily
News Archive/Todd Maisel, 74; Newscom: Everett Collection/Augie Rose, 65, MCT/Todd
Sumlin, 104, PacificCoastNews, 92, Reuters/Brendan McDermid, 13, Reuters/Chip East,
26, Reuters/Mike Segar, 7, Reuters/Pool/Seth Wenig, 11, Sipa USA/Safety Reliability
Methods, 97, Splash News/J.B. Nicholas, 98–99, Splash News/
NY Post, 54, Splash News/Steven Day, 52–53, Splash News/Turner, 83, Wenn/Carrie
Devorah, 38, Zuma Press/Bryan Smith, 63, Zuma Press/Mariela Lombard, 79, Zuma
Press/Sharkpixs, 67, Zuma Press/Trevor Collens, 43; Reuters: Brendan McDermid, 58,
Eric Thayer, 57, 76, Gary Hershorn, 68; Shutterstock: EQRoy, 33, Everett Collection, 4,
Kathy Hutchins, 100, Kent Sievers, 25, rck_953, 20; Wikimedia: National Transportation
Safety Board, 87

TABLE OF
CONTENTS

A huge Chicago crowd cheered the Obama family on election night, but Barack Obama would face major challenges as president.

FOREWORD

As 2009 dawned, many Americans were less than enthusiastic about the new year. Newly elected President Barack Obama promised a bright new beginning. But he was leading a nation faced with serious challenges. The national economy was stalled. Unemployment had risen to 7.6 percent, with 11.6 million Americans out of work.

There was also difficulty on the international front. The United States was engaged in two wars against terrorists and the governments that supported them in Afghanistan and Iraq. President George W. Bush (2001–2009) had initiated the wars, both of which had become politically controversial in the United States. Other armed conflicts were underway in Israel, India, and Sri Lanka.

Many Americans planned to escape their troubles with midwinter vacations. Some packed their cars or boarded planes to travel around the country to be with family and friends. Others, immersed in business, flew to distant cities to attend meetings and conferences.

On the morning of Thursday, January 15, New Yorkers awoke to snow showers that ended by late morning. It was the coldest day of winter so far, with temperatures 12 degrees below normal for that time of year. The forecast looked like bad news for those planning to travel.

Although it was not a great day for flying, thousands of travelers headed to the three major New York City-area airports. Before long LaGuardia and the region's other airports were bustling with people of all ages and backgrounds. Passengers, airport workers, and air travel employees went about their business, preparing for another busy day.

Among the flights scheduled that day at LaGuardia Airport, which is located in the city's borough of Queens, was US Airways Flight 1549. The flight was scheduled from New York to Charlotte, North Carolina, and then to Seattle, Washington. Normally a routine flight, on this day it would be anything but ordinary.

Snow and cold temperatures greeted pedestrians in Times Square on January 15, 2009, a typically busy day at the major airports serving the city. Winter in New York City often brings snow and cold that can hamper travel in and out of the area, which attracts millions of tourists and businesspeople each year.

"WHY ARE YOU GOING DOWN THERE TODAY?"

1

The air temperature in New York City was just under 20 degrees Fahrenheit when US Airways Flight 1549 took off.

Lucille Palmer

Goshen, New York
January 15, 2009, 10:00 a.m.

Eighty-five-year-old Lucille Palmer was looking forward to flying to Charlotte, North Carolina, to see her great-grandson. She would be there to celebrate his first birthday. So she was not happy when her son called and told her he didn't like the idea.

"Why are you going down there today?" he said. "The weather is terrible."

It was true that it was midwinter and very cold. But Palmer assured him that the flight would be safe and she would be fine. Besides that, her daughter Diane was going with her. Her son grudgingly dropped the subject and ended the conversation.

"Your brother is such a worrywart," said Palmer to her daughter as she hung up the phone. "A little snow isn't going to scare off this senior."

Diane smiled. "Let's go, Mom," she said. "The limo is here."

Chesley "Sully" Sullenberger

LaGuardia Airport, Queens, New York
January 15, 2009, 12:00 p.m.

Captain Chesley "Sully" Sullenberger greeted his copilot, Jeff Skiles, and the three flight attendants as he boarded the US Airways Airbus A320. He hadn't flown with Skiles before, but that was no surprise. Pilots and copilots on commercial airlines were often paired with people they didn't know. Skiles had only a decade's flying experience compared to Sullenberger's 30-year career as a commercial pilot. Skiles had a professional but friendly manner, and Sullenberger decided they'd get along fine for the flight to Charlotte, North Carolina.

In the cockpit Sullenberger looked up at the

Sully Sullenberger (left) and copilot Jeff Skiles

clouded sky. He noticed the sun was starting
to break through the clouds. The morning's
thin carpet of snow had been cleared from the
runways. The plane had arrived about 40 minutes
behind schedule due to deicing at Pittsburgh,
Pennsylvania, its previous point of departure.
Sullenberger felt sure they would make up some of
the lost time once they were in the air. This would
be just another routine flight, one of thousands he
had made for US Airways.

Tess Sosa

LaGuardia Airport, Queens, New York
January 15, 2009, 1:40 p.m.

"Isn't he the cutest little baby?" said an older woman to Tess Sosa.

"And he's wearing the cutest little boots," said her companion.

Forty-year-old Sosa smiled and shifted Damian, her 9-month-old baby, in her arms. Her husband, Martin, stood next to her in line with their 4-year-old daughter, Sofia. He didn't look happy. For 15 minutes, security officials had gone through their luggage, inspecting every jar of baby food they were carrying. Now they were rushing to get on board Flight 1549, where they faced another challenge. The couple and Sofia had not been assigned side-by-side seats. Sosa hoped they could find two people to switch seats to allow her family to be together on the plane. At the front of the line, a US Airways employee assured them they would have plenty of time to get settled.

Tess Sosa and her daughter, Sofia

"The flight is delayed," she told them in a pleasant voice. "We won't be taking off for a while yet."

Sosa felt hopeful that the extra time would allow them to find passengers willing to switch seats with them. She didn't want to face this flight alone with Damian in her lap.

Eric Stevenson

Seat 12F, US Airways Airbus A320
January 15, 2009, 2:45 p.m.

Forty-five-year-old accountant Eric Stevenson settled into his first-class seat on the plane. He felt fortunate. His flight to Charlotte on another airline had been canceled due to weather. He had just managed to get a seat on Flight 1549. Now he looked forward to a short and relaxing flight after his busy business trip in New York City.

Tess Sosa

Seat 19E, US Airways Airbus A320
January 15, 2009, 2:55 p.m.

Sosa was relieved to see a young man switch seats with Martin so he could sit next to Sofia. But when she tried to find someone to switch with her, no one was willing. Now she would be separated from her husband and daughter. Feeling her anxiety level rising, Sosa turned to a passing flight attendant.

"Can't you do something so I can sit with my family?" she asked.

The attendant leaned over to speak to Sosa. "I can't order people to change their seats," she said.

Sosa was not prepared to accept this. She unbuckled her seat belt as the plane pulled away from the gate.

"Sit back down," the attendant said in a stern voice.

Sosa did as she was told. She was grateful that Damian was staying calm in her arms. This was more than she could say for herself.

Doreen Welsh

Cabin, US Airways Airbus A320
January 15, 2009, 3:00 p.m.

Thirty-nine-year-old flight attendant Doreen Welsh felt some sympathy for the anxious woman with the baby. Still, she knew she could do nothing to help her. There was no point in trying to persuade passengers to change seats if they weren't willing. She continued her walk down the central aisle, checking that everyone had his or her seat belt buckled. Another woman stopped her as she passed.

"Is this your first flight today?" she asked nervously.

Welsh smiled and nodded.

"How are the skies? Will they be bumpy?" the woman continued.

Welsh's smile widened. She had confronted this type of passenger many times in her 10 years as a flight attendant. These passengers' fear of flying was tangible, and winter weather only made it worse.

"I don't like to fly," the woman admitted. "I'm a little nervous."

"Don't worry," Welsh assured her. "Flying makes me nervous too."

Sully Sullenberger

Cockpit, US Airways Airbus A320
January 15, 2009, 3:22 p.m.

Flight 1549 was 11th in line for takeoff. The delay had given Sullenberger and Skiles some time to go over the controls and get to know each other a little better. Sullenberger rechecked the manifest. There were 155 people aboard—150 passengers and five crew members, including the three flight attendants. Now Sullenberger let Skiles take the controls as they made final preparations for takeoff.

Patrick Harten

Westbury, Long Island, New York
January 15, 2009, 3:25 p.m.

As the plane rolled down the runway, the LaGuardia controller passed radio communications to the New York Terminal Radar Approach Control at Westbury, Long Island.

Air traffic controller Patrick Harten, age 34, had been assigned to the plane's position 14 minutes earlier and was ready. He listened to the pilot's first communication, "Cactus fifteen forty-nine, seven hundred climbing five thousand." The pilot was telling him the plane was at an elevation of 700 feet and was climbing to 5,000 feet.

"Cactus fifteen forty-nine," responded Harten, "New York departure radar contact, climb and maintain one five thousand." He was telling the pilot it was safe for him to climb to 15,000 feet.

Sully Sullenberger

Cockpit, US Airways Airbus A320
January 15, 2009, 3:26 p.m.

As the Airbus soared into the now-bright blue skies, Sullenberger looked through his window at the river directly below.

"What a beautiful view of the Hudson," he said.

"Yeah," replied Skiles as he continued to accelerate upward.

"MAYDAY! MAYDAY! MAYDAY!"

A flock of Canada geese crossed the flight path of US Airways Flight 1549.

Jeff Skiles

Cockpit, US Airways Airbus A320
January 15, 2009, 3:27:11 p.m.

Copilot Skiles was the first to see them—a flock of Canada geese in a V-shaped flight formation coming toward the plane. For an

instant he thought they would miss colliding with the birds. But then came the awful thud as the bodies of geese pelted the plane's hard surface.

"Birds!" cried Sullenberger.

"Whoa!" said Skiles, as the plane shook from the impact.

"Oh, yeah," Sullenberger replied.

An awful odor of jet fuel mixed with burning bird flesh filled Skiles's nostrils. Then he heard the engines suddenly go quiet. "Uh-oh," he said.

"We got one roll . . . ," said Sullenberger. "Both of 'em rolling back."

Skiles knew he was referring to their two engines shutting down. This was bad.

"My airplane," snapped Sullenberger, and Skiles turned over control of the plane to him.

Doreen Welsh

Flight attendant Welsh was in the cabin's aisle checking the overhead storage bins when she felt the impact. She saw a woman in Seat 26D in the rear unbuckle her seat belt and start moving toward her. "Do you want me to call for help?" the woman asked.

"No. Sit back down," Welsh ordered. She told the woman to take the middle seat, which was vacant. This way if she needed to sit fast, she could take the woman's aisle seat.

It occurred to Welsh that they might have hit some birds. It happened occasionally and the results were rarely serious. She just hoped the birds' body parts hadn't clogged one of the engines and shut it down. Then they would have to return to LaGuardia. And after the long delay to get into the air, that would make no one happy.

Andrew Gray

Seat 14F, US Airways Airbus A320
January 15, 2009, 3:27:16 p.m.

U.S. Army Captain Andrew Gray felt the thuds and could smell a terrible odor. Sitting next to him was his fiancé, Stephanie King. The two had met through an online dating service while he was stationed in Italy. Now their wedding was only weeks away and they were flying to his home in Fayetteville, North Carolina. A smoky haze filled the cabin, and Gray heard someone in the rear of the plane cry out, "Fire!" Stephanie tightened her grip on his hand.

"What's happening?" she asked.

"I don't know," he said. He suddenly felt incredibly helpless. This was a rare feeling for him and he didn't like it. He had only recently returned from a tour in Afghanistan, where he led soldiers into battle against the Taliban. But now he could think of nothing to do to protect the woman he loved.

"Andrew, what's happening?" she repeated, her eyes filled with fear.

He put his arm around her shoulder and tried to sound reassuring. "Don't worry, don't worry," he said. "We just blew a fuse." He silently prayed that he was right.

Sully Sullenberger

Cockpit, US Airways Airbus A320
January 15, 2009, 3:27:15 p.m.

Sullenberger had never experienced a bird strike before in his long flying career. But he knew they were almost always minor mishaps. The worst result he had heard about from a bird strike was a plane losing power in one engine. This had forced the pilot to make an unscheduled landing. But now it was clear that Sullenberger's plane had lost power in both engines. They needed to land, and fast.

"Mayday! Mayday! Mayday!" he said into his radio, repeating the emergency distress signal. "Uh, this is, uh, Cactus fifteen thirty-nine. Hit birds. We've lost thrust in both engines. We're turning back towards LaGuardia."

According to the Federal Aviation Administration, more than 90 percent of bird strikes occur at or below 3,500 feet above ground level. Flight 1549 had climbed to about 2,800 feet before it struck the passing birds.

The voice of the controller from Westbury, Long Island, came crackling over the radio. "OK, uh, you need to return to LaGuardia? Turn left heading of, uh, two two zero."

Air traffic control at LaGuardia Airport communicated with controller Patrick Harten, who hoped to send Flight 1549 safely back to the airport.

Patrick Harten

Westbury, Long Island, New York
January 15, 2009, 3:27:35 p.m.

Harten had assisted pilots after bird strikes 15 times in his 10-year career in air traffic control. He was proud of the fact that he had guided each one safely back to land and had never lost a plane. He didn't intend to change that record now. He immediately contacted the control tower at LaGuardia.

"Tower," he said, "stop your departures. We got an emergency returning."

"Who is it?" replied the LaGuardia controller.

"It's fifteen twenty-nine," replied Harten. He wasn't sure if under stress he had gotten the flight number wrong, but that hardly mattered. "Bird strike. He lost all engines. He lost the thrust in the engines. He is returning immediately."

There was a brief pause on the other end. "Cactus fifteen twenty-nine," repeated the controller. "Which engine?"

"He lost thrust in both engines," Harten repeated.

"Got it," came the reply.

Emma Cowan

Emma Cowan heard a strange sound, like a loud pop outside the plane. A native of Perth, Australia, she was used to long flights and air turbulence. But this sounded like something quite different, as if something had actually struck the plane.

An aspiring singer and songwriter, Cowan performed under the name Sophina. She had flown to the United States for a vacation. Unlike many New Yorkers, she enjoyed the cold winter weather. It was a refreshing change from the intense heat of summer back home in Australia's southern hemisphere. Now she was looking forward to visiting her Aussie friends living in Charlotte. Then she smelled a horrible smell— like burnt flesh. She began to feel uneasy for the first time on her American vacation.

Joe Hart

Seat 7B, US Airways Airbus A320
January 15, 2009, 3:27:40 p.m.

Joe Hart, 50, a sales representative from Cornelius, North Carolina, heard a thud. He called out to a friend who was sitting a few rows away, "This can't be good."

Hart looked out the window and saw the rooftops of tall Manhattan buildings. Then he noticed that the rooftops appeared to be rising as the plane lost altitude. He amended his statement: "This definitely can't be good." He felt the plane banking hard to the left. The Hudson River was below them. *If we hit the water, the plane will break apart and no one will survive,* he thought.

Eric Stevenson

Seat 12F, US Airways Airbus A320
January 15, 2009, 3:27:45 p.m.

Stevenson was beginning to think that the good luck that got him on this plane might be running out. He looked out over the plane's wing and could see birds being sucked into the engine. They came out the other end as brown smoke. It was a startling sight.

Now he could feel the plane descending rapidly. It brought back bad memories. Twenty-two years earlier, Stevenson had been on a Boeing 767 flying over the Pacific Ocean. The pilot had accidentally turned off the engines, and the plane plunged downward. It was only a little more than a minute before the pilot was able to restart the engines. However, it seemed like an eternity to Stevenson and the other passengers. The plane had pulled up only 500 feet above the water.

It had been a traumatic, life-altering experience for Stevenson. He'd left the United States and moved to Paris, France, where he still lived.

Oh my god, he thought, feeling the plane continue to fall. *It was only supposed to be a once-in-a-lifetime event and here it is happening all over again.*

sully sullenberger

Cockpit, US Airways Airbus A320
January 15, 2009, 3:28 p.m.

Sullenberger watched as Skiles quickly pulled out the correct checklist from the reference handbook. *This can't be happening,* he thought. *This doesn't happen to me.* But it was happening, and he had to make a swift decision to avoid a crash landing. He knew from years of training and experience that he didn't have enough altitude or speed to turn the plane around. He couldn't make it back to LaGuardia. He had to find a closer place to land safely.

The air controller at Westbury was back on the radio.

"Cactus fifteen twenty-nine, if we can get it for you, do you want to try to land runway one three?" Harten asked, again misstating the flight number.

"We're unable," Sullenberger replied. "We may end up in the Hudson."

There was brief silence on the other end.

"All right, Cactus fifteen forty-nine," the controller said. "Go for runway three one."

It was as if he hadn't heard what Sullenberger said or didn't want to hear it. "Unable," replied the pilot.

"OK, what do you need to land?" the controller asked.

"I'm not sure we can make any runway," said Sullenberger. "What's over to our right? Anything in New Jersey, maybe Teterboro?" He knew Teterboro Airport was a small airport only a few miles away on the New Jersey side of the Hudson.

"You wanna try and go to Teterboro?" said the controller.

"Yes," Sullenberger said.

But even as the word left his mouth, Sullenberger knew it was impossible. They'd never make it the short distance to Teterboro. They'd crash before getting there. He had only two choices left. He could land on the roadways, but in New York City this seemed extremely unsafe. The plane would likely crash into an overpass or be forced to land on top of driving cars. Both people on the plane and motorists would almost certainly be killed. His other choice was to land on the Hudson River. It was clear of people and boats as far as he could see. He had to go for the river. It was their only hope.

An aerial view of Teterboro Airport in New Jersey, which might have provided a landing place for Flight 1549. If the plane had come up short of the runway, however, a devastating crash seemed a certain result.

"BRACE FOR IMPACT!"

3

A view of the Hudson River south of the George Washington Bridge, which Flight 1549 passed near on its way toward the water.

Sully Sullenberger

Cockpit, US Airways Airbus A320
January 15, 2009, 3:29 p.m.

He had made his decision. They would take their chances in the water. There was really no other alternative. Sullenberger felt OK, even calm and confident, about his decision. Now he had to let the rest of the people aboard know. There was no time for lengthy explanations or detailed instructions.

"This is the captain," he said into his intercom. "Brace for impact!"

Lucille Palmer

Seat 17F, US Airways Airbus A320
January 15, 2009, 3:29:15 p.m.

As the pilot's voice filled the cabin, Palmer turned to her daughter, Diane.

"What'd he say?" she asked. "We're going down?"

"No, Ma," said Diane.

But Palmer could see the uncertainty and fear in her daughter's face. Oddly enough, she felt no fear, just a numbness. It was all happening too quickly for her to process. She refused to look out the window. She hugged Diane tightly as they leaned forward in their seats.

John Howell

Seat 2D, US Airways Airbus A320
January 15, 2009, 3:29:16 p.m.

Accountant John Howell listened as the flight attendants echoed the pilot's words, crying, "Brace! Brace! Heads down! Stay down!" He caught the eye of one attendant standing near him. The look she returned said that everything was going to be fine. Then he looked out the window at the waters of the Hudson rising up toward the falling plane. He knew that everything wasn't going to be fine.

Howell cinched his seat belt as tight as he could, leaned forward, and grabbed his ankles

Captain Sullenberger's plane (circled, upper right) descends past Midtown Manhattan moments before reaching the water.

with both hands. As he sat there, hunched, listening to the cries and prayers of other passengers, he thought back. Seven years before, his brother George, a firefighter, had died in the terrorist attack on September 11, 2001. George died a hero at the site of the World Trade Center towers. His body was never recovered from the rubble.

George's death had been devastating for Howell's family, especially his parents. Now, seven years later, he was about to die as well. It didn't seem fair. He was furious with himself. *I didn't have to have this job,* he thought. *I didn't have to be going down in an airplane in New York.* Just before the plane hit the water he thought, *If I go down, my mother's not going to survive this.*

Patrick Harten

Patrick Harten

Westbury, Long Island, New York January 15, 2009, 3:29:21 p.m.

"Cactus fifteen twenty-nine, turn right two eight zero, you can land runway one at Teterboro," said Harten into his radio.

"We can't do it," came back the clipped reply.

"OK," said the controller. "Which runway would you like at Teterboro?"

"We're gonna be in the Hudson," the pilot replied.

"I'm sorry. Say again, Cactus?" asked Harten, not understanding. Once he understood, he wished he didn't. Nearly 20 seconds passed. They seemed like an eternity to Harten. "Cactus fifteen forty-nine, radar contact is lost, you also got Newark Airport off your two o'clock in about seven miles," he said. More precious seconds passed in silence. "Cactus fifteen twenty-nine, uh, you still on?"

Harten repeated the information about a runway available at Newark, but he heard nothing more from Flight 1549. He had lost radio contact and could only assume the worst. The plane must have gone into the Hudson.

Andrew Gray

Seat 14F, US Airways Airbus A320
January 15, 2009, 3:30 p.m.

The pilot's words had confirmed Gray's worst fears. They were gliding in the air without power and were about to crash into the Hudson River. All his words of comfort to Stephanie were empty. He could clearly see the panic in her eyes. Gray could only hope that they didn't lose consciousness on impact and could swim out of the fallen plane.

Taking Stephanie's hand he murmured, "Babe, I love you."

"I love you too," she replied, and they kissed.

Then they both prayed aloud. "Lord," Gray said, "please help deliver us and get us out of this mess somehow."

Tess Sosa

Seat 19E, US Airways Airbus A320
January 15, 2009, 3:30:05 p.m.

Sosa was torn. A few rows ahead, she could hear her daughter, Sofia, crying. She tried to comfort her, while at the same time deciding how to brace herself. She didn't want to accidentally injure Damian, who was sitting in her lap. The man sitting next to them offered to help. He had been kind and reassuring while they were still on the runway. Now he was willing to hold her baby. She believed Damian would be safe in this man's hands.

"Are you sure?" said the man, as Sosa held out her son for him to take.

"Absolutely," she said.

She watched as he carefully took Damian and held him the long way from arm to arm. He put one knee on the back of the seat ahead of him and pushed back hard in his seat. Sosa braced herself, but never took her eyes off Damian.

Eric Stevenson

Seat 12F, US Airways Airbus A320
January 15, 2009, 3:30:15 p.m.

Before he followed the attendants' commands and braced for impact, Stevenson took a business card from his pocket. "Mom and Jane, I love you," he wrote on it to his mother and sister. Then he put the card into his right front pants pocket. If this was indeed the end of his life, at least he would leave a message to his loved ones. He put his arms on the seat in front of him and placed his head on them. It suddenly occurred to him that the note might be separated from his body if the cabin came apart. It might never be found. The thought saddened him.

Emma Cowan

Emma Cowan

Seat 13F, US Airways Airbus A320
January 15, 2009, 3:30:15 p.m.

Like so many of the other passengers, Cowan
hugged the seat in front of her and prayed. Was she
really going to die like this, thousands of miles from

her homeland? She struggled to reconcile herself with death. There was a sudden jolt and it felt as if the plane had slammed into a building.

"OK," she thought. "I'm going to heaven now."

Jeff Skiles

Cockpit, US Airways Airbus A320
January 15, 2009, 3:30:15 p.m.

Skiles's ears filled with the automatic callouts from the Enhanced Ground Proximity Warning System (EGPWS). "Pull up, pull up, pull up, pull up," a recorded voice repeated. "Pull up, pull up, pull up, pull up." But they couldn't pull up. They were plunging quickly toward the water. Even though they hadn't hit the water yet, it felt as if they were sinking into a bathtub filled with ice water.

Now the Flight Warning Computer was chiming madly and the EGPWS was crying, "Caution terrain!"

"Got any ideas?" asked Sullenberger as they continued to lose altitude.

"Actually not," replied Skiles.

The EGPWS had only one idea and it kept repeating it: "Terrain, terrain. Pull up, pull up, pull up."

"We're gonna brace," said Sullenberger.

"EVACUATE!"

4

The crew of US Airways Flight 1549 had to move quickly to get passengers out of the cabin and onto the wings of the floating plane.

Sully Sullenberger

Cockpit, US Airways Airbus A320
January 15, 2009, 3:30:43 p.m.

The plane met the river slightly nose-up. Sullenberger could feel the Airbus's rear hit the water hard. The captain felt a sharp jolt on impact. In seconds the aircraft came to a standstill, floating on the river. It was a rough but solid landing. Sullenberger turned to Skiles and they both spoke at the same time: "That wasn't as bad as I thought."

There was no screaming or yelling from the passenger cabin, just the sound of muffled talking. That was good. But they weren't out of danger yet. They now had to get all 155 people off the plane as quickly as possible. It might be only minutes before the aircraft sank to the bottom of the Hudson.

There were exit doors at the front, middle, and back of the plane. Once opened, the exits would automatically deploy inflatable slides. The slides could then be detached and become life rafts for the passengers. As Skiles raced through the evacuation checklist, a necessary protocol, Sullenberger opened the cockpit door. He faced the passengers and attendants for the first time. "Evacuate!" he cried.

John Howell

Seat 2D, US Airways Airbus A320
January 15, 2009, 3:30:45 p.m.

Howell could feel the plane's tail drag in the water. It made a horrible sound. *It's going to come apart,* he thought. He imagined the water rushing through the cabin and drowning them all. He thought about his poor mother.

He was interrupted by the flight attendants. "Don life vests! Come this way!" they shouted.

Howell grabbed the life vest under his seat and rushed forward to the nearby front exit. Once out of the plane, he stepped with other first-class passengers into an inflatable slide-raft already deployed in the water. He shivered in the cold January air and looked around at the familiar Manhattan skyline. He was overcome with gratitude. *How did this come about?* he thought. *How come I'm alive? How did this miraculous thing happen?*

Lucille Palmer

Seat 17F, US Airways Airbus A320
January 15, 2009, 3:31 p.m.

Palmer watched in confusion as people rushed past her and Diane. They were climbing over seats like a herd of stampeding animals. She didn't know how she would get off the plane and could only think of her daughter.

"Just leave me," she told Diane.

"Ma!" cried Diane.

Seconds passed as people continued to push past them. Palmer looked down. The water, just an inch or two on the floor a moment ago, was now nearly up to her knees. Suddenly she felt a strong hand grip her shirt. A middle-aged man was pushing her forward down the aisle. "The crowd will move you along," he told her, letting go of her shirt.

Diane was following close behind Palmer. Then all at once she saw the smiling face of a flight attendant.

"I was worried about you," the attendant said to the mother and daughter. Then she guided them through one of the middle exits over the wing and into a life raft.

Doreen Welsh

Cabin, US Airways Airbus A320
January 15, 2009, 3:31 p.m.

Welsh was sitting in a rear jump seat when the plane hit the water. She didn't have a window to look out to see what happened. She thought perhaps they had landed back at LaGuardia. But the water surging through the broken rear exit door told her differently. The cold water quickly rose to her armpits.

People rushed toward her to get out the rear,

but there was no way out here. The door was jammed with water rushing under it. Because of this, Welsh assumed that the rear rafts would not deploy. This would mean there would not be enough room on the remaining rafts, and passengers would have to stand on the wings.

"Turn around!" she cried to the panicking passengers. "Go to the front! You can't get out here! You have two minutes!" The ideal time to evacuate a plane in a dangerous situation was 90 seconds. Welsh doubted they could empty the plane that fast.

As she waded through the rising water, she felt a falling object strike her leg. In all the chaos of the evacuation, she paid it little attention.

Eric Stevenson

Seat 12F, US Airways Airbus A320
January 15, 2009, 3:31:30 p.m.

To his amazement, Stevenson realized he wasn't going to die after all. It seemed he would survive another plane crash.

Passengers huddled on the wings of the plane while awaiting rescue. The water of the Hudson River was brutally cold, and the air temperature was in the teens.

He went out the nearby wing exit. He joined passengers standing on the plane's left wing because the raft below was filled. In landing, the plane seemed to have tilted to the right. The left wing was now lifted out of the water. This was good because it meant Stevenson would stay dry longer. But it was also bad. Stevenson and others

on the wing were having a difficult time keeping their balance because of the steep angle. If they slipped they would fall off the wing into the Hudson's icy waters.

Stevenson kneeled down to keep his balance. It was then, to his astonishment, that he saw people in the water splashing around. He wondered if they had fallen from the wing or had deliberately jumped into the water.

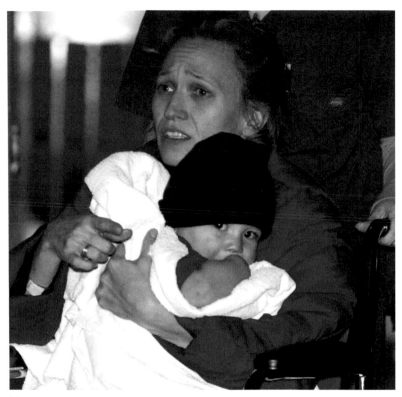

Tess Sosa and her son, Damian

Tess Sosa

Seat 19E, US Airways Airbus A320
January 15, 2009, 3:32 p.m.

For a terrifying moment, Sosa didn't know what to do. She was separated from her husband and daughter, four rows behind her. The kind man sitting next to her who had handed Damian back to her after they hit the water was gone. She watched, her baby in her arms, as people rushed by them down the aisle.

Desperate to escape the sinking plane, she began climbing over the seats, moving awkwardly while holding Damian in her arms. Suddenly she came face-to-face with a young man. He grabbed her and Damian and lifted them into the air. "You're coming with me," he said. He carried them all the way to the front exit. In seconds, Martin and Sofia joined her there.

Emma Cowan

Seat 13F, US Airways Airbus A320
January 15, 2009, 3:32:10 p.m.

Cowan grabbed a life vest and followed the stampede to an exit. The evacuation struck her as somehow both orderly and messy all at once.

Reaching the exit, she bumped her head on the door. As she stepped out of the plane the icy air shocked her. That's when she remembered that her luggage and passport were still on the plane.

Sully Sullenberger

Cabin, US Airways Airbus A320
January 15, 2009, 3:32:20 p.m.

Sullenberger was relieved to see that nearly everyone was off the plane. All evacuees were either crowded together in one of the inflatable rafts or standing on one of the wings. The right wing was low in the water. Sullenberger knew it might take a while for rescue boats to arrive. He also knew that the cold air would be intense. The captain, Skiles, and a few remaining passengers gathered up coats and blankets for passengers on the wings. They also scooped up any life vests and jackets they found for those who had left them behind. The rear of the plane was steadily sinking into the river. The water throughout the cabin was now almost up to their waists.

After gathering what they could, the remaining passengers exited. Only Sullenberger, Skiles, and flight attendant Donna Dent remained aboard.

"It's time to go!" cried Dent. "We've got to get off this plane!"

Passenger Emma Cowan (center) was among those in a life raft awaiting rescuers.

"I'm coming," said Sullenberger. But he had one last thing to do. He went back to the cockpit to get his overcoat and the air maintenance logbook. He tossed his coat to a shivering male passenger in the left-front raft. Then, seeing that Skiles and Dent had exited, he looked over the plane one last time. He wanted to make certain there was no one left on board.

"THROW THE BABY!"

5

The 155 people on board the Airbus had to hurry onto the wings and emergency rafts as cold river water rose in the plane's cabin.

Tess Sosa

US Airways Airbus A320
January 15, 2009, 3:32:30 p.m.

Sosa looked down from the exit door at the inflated slide-raft below, filled with passengers. She froze. She didn't see how she could go down onto the raft. What if she lost hold of Damian as she climbed down? What if he fell into the icy river water and drowned? What if they both fell off the raft? Martin, standing next to her with Sofia, looked just as helpless.

Women on the raft saw her predicament and thought they had the answer. "Throw the baby!" several of them shouted up at her.

Throw her baby? Never! she thought.

A man yelled at her to come back into the plane and go out another way. But Sosa didn't trust any of them. Then a woman approached her quietly from the wing. "Give me your baby," she said.

It was strange, but something about this woman made Sosa trust her. Maybe it was the tone of her voice or the gentle look in her eyes. She seemed to understand. She handed Damian to the woman, who in turn gave him to a man on the raft. Then the woman asked to take Sofia. Sosa handed Sofia over, and the woman sat down on the raft and placed the girl on her lap.

Sosa watched Damian's progress from passenger to passenger in the raft. He ended up in the arms of a large, tall man. Then Sosa managed to get down into the raft. Sofia joined her there. Someone passed the baby back to Sosa. Damian, wearing a diaper and a T-shirt, smiled up at her. Tears came to her eyes. Then she looked up at the plane's right wing and saw her husband standing there, waist-deep in water.

Lucille Palmer

Hudson River, New York
January 15, 2009, 3:32:45 p.m.

Palmer had never felt so vulnerable and helpless. She sat next to her daughter in a raft, her lips trembling and her thin body shaking from the bitter cold. A man near her took off his sweatshirt and wrapped it around her. Then he hugged her. His body and the sweatshirt felt warm and comforting.

Emma Cowan

US Airways Airbus A320
January 15, 2009, 3:32:50 p.m.

On the raft Cowan could only think about one thing—her passport. Without it, how would she get out of the country and back to Australia? She had to get it.

"I have to get on the plane," she told the woman next to her. This woman tried to calm her down. "You can't go back," she said. "The plane isn't safe."

"But you don't understand," Cowan responded. "I must get my passport. I am not from here. Let me back on the plane. I don't live in this country."

"Calm down," the woman said. "People will help you." Cowan wasn't buying it, but the people around her would not let her go back to the exit door. She had no choice but to remain where she was.

Remington Chin

US Airways Airbus A320
January 15, 2009, 3:32:55 p.m.

Twenty-five-year-old Remington Chin saw the rafts as he exited the plane. Still, he felt he'd be safer getting as far away from the plane as he could. After all, he reasoned, it could explode. So he jumped into the water. Lean and athletic, Chin felt he could swim the short distance to the Manhattan side of the Hudson.

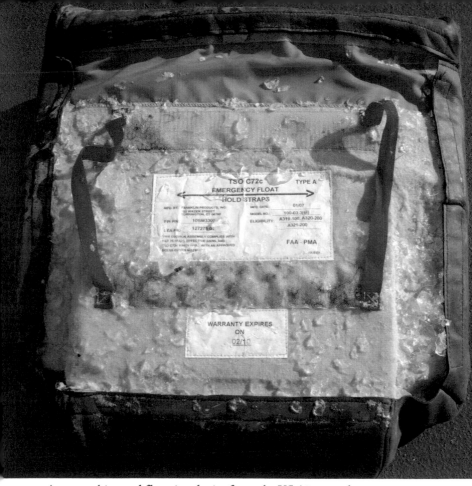

A seat cushion and flotation device from the US Airways plane was recovered from the Hudson River.

The water was like ice. He clung to the seat cushion he had grabbed in the plane. Although he excelled in several sports, swimming wasn't one of them. In fact, he had almost drowned once. But he felt he could make it to shore despite that.

He turned to look back one last time at the plane. A man in the raft was waving at him, urging him to come back. If the man had been dressed casually like a passenger, Chin would have ignored him. But he was wearing a white shirt and a green tie. He looked like someone in authority, someone worth paying attention to.

This guy works for the airline, Chin thought. *He knows more than I do.* He turned and swam back to the raft. Someone pulled him in. It turned out the man waving to him was just another passenger, not a crew member. Then Chin saw a rescue boat approaching the raft and knew he had made the right decision.

Doreen Welsh

Hudson River, New York
January 15, 2009, 3:33 p.m.

Welsh was grateful to the passenger—he said his name was Douglas—for helping her into the raft. As he put her down, they both looked at his blood-covered shirt. Welsh realized in horror that it was her blood.

Doreen Welsh

"Where are you injured?" Douglas asked her.

"I don't know," she said, feeling stupid. She pulled up her pants leg and noticed an ugly gash on her leg. Then she remembered something had hit her in the cabin after the crash. Douglas had her raise her bleeding leg onto a stack of seat cushions. Then a doctor and nurse, also passengers in the raft, made a simple tourniquet. They wrapped it around her leg to stop the bleeding. Welsh tried to thank them, but she was crying so much that she couldn't speak.

Andrew Gray

US Airways Airbus A320
January 15, 2009, 3:33:10 p.m.

Gray and his fiancé, Stephanie, weren't able to get into the right-wing raft because it was already full. They stood on the wing, the water up to their ankles and rising quickly. "Don't worry," Gray kept telling her over and over, "boats are coming."

In truth, he didn't see any boats coming to their rescue. But he knew they had to be on their way. This was New York, a huge city filled with experienced first responders. As he held Stephanie, Gray could feel the water creeping up his leg.

The aircraft took on water and sank lower and lower into the river while commercial and emergency watercraft rushed to aid the plane's passengers and crew.

The ferry *Thomas Jefferson* inched near the plane to help passengers off the wing.

"RESCUE PEOPLE ON THE WINGS FIRST!"

Vince Lombardi

Hudson River, New York
January 15, 2009, 3:34 p.m.

Captain Vince Lombardi of the ferry *Thomas Jefferson* was pulling out of Pier 79 at West 39th Street in Manhattan when he saw the plane. It was floating in the water, not far from his boat. He immediately changed course. Abandoning his regular route, he made a beeline for the plane. In just a few minutes, his was the first ferry to reach the scene.

Lombardi and most of his crew had been trained to conduct a rescue operation. Now they were going to get a chance to put that training into action. As they neared the plane, Lombardi could see dozens of passengers standing on the wings.

69

Ferry Captain Vince Lombardi

He sailed toward the right wing until the two crafts were only about 10 feet apart. That was as close as he dared to get. He feared the motion of the boat might tip the plane and send people into the water. Several deckhands lowered a metal ladder down the side of the boat.

"Come on!" the captain cried to the people standing on the right wing. Nobody moved. Were they waiting for him to come and get them?

"Come on!" he yelled again, louder this time.

Finally, a young woman dived into the icy water and swam the short distance to the ladder. She grabbed onto it and then froze.

"Let's go!" cried a deckhand.

"I'm stuck," said the poor woman. But she suddenly started to scramble up the ladder. In a few seconds she was aboard, wet and shivering. Lombardi was pleased to see the ferry passengers quickly surround her. Someone gave her a hat to wear; someone else gave her a pair of gloves. Two men took off their coats and draped them over her. A woman even gave her a cell phone so she could call her loved ones.

Lombardi smiled. It took a disaster like this to bring out the best in people. Then he turned his attention back to the wing. One person after another was diving into the water and going for the ladder.

Sully Sullenberger

As Sullenberger climbed into the raft, he noticed it was not filled. Many other passengers were on the wings and the rafts on the other side of the plane. He hoped that everyone was accounted for. At the very least he was certain there was no one left inside the sinking plane.

Several rescue boats were already arriving on the scene. A wave of relief washed over him. One boat—he could see it was the *Athena* from the bold letters written on its side—approached.

Sullenberger knew the people on the wing needed to be rescued before those in the raft. The wings were slick with water and on a steep angle. The people on them were in greater danger of falling into the river.

"Rescue people on the wings first!" he cried to the approaching crew above the noise of the ferry engines. Not a single person in the raft objected. As they waited Sullenberger tried to get a head count of the people in the raft and on the wing. But with so much chaos around him, his efforts were in vain.

Andrew Gray

US Airways Airbus A320
January 15, 2009, 3:37 p.m.

"Go! Go! Climb the thing!" Gray cried to Stephanie, who was frozen on the ladder of the *Thomas Jefferson*. In another few seconds, she scrambled up and was helped aboard by two deckhands. There were four or five people between Gray and Stephanie, and he waited his turn to get onto the ladder.

Once aboard, he quickly found Stephanie and wrapped his arms around her shivering body. Then Gray suddenly realized he needed to get word to his family. He pulled out his cell phone and found that it was still working. He punched the buttons. "Hey, first of all, we're OK," he told his parents when they answered. "We've been in a plane crash. Turn on the news. Gotta go." Then he hung up and held Stephanie tighter.

Stephanie King and Andrew Gray, survivors of Flight 1549

Sully Sullenberger

Hudson River, New York
January 15, 2009, 3:38 p.m.

Sullenberger sat, clipboard in hand, and waited patiently as the *Athena* rescued all the people on the left wing. A young man in a college sweatshirt moved closer to him. Sullenberger had not identified himself and didn't know if anyone would recognize him. But this fellow clearly did.

"I owe you my life," he said.

Sullenberger felt almost embarrassed at the attention. "It was just my job," he said. "We were very fortunate."

But the young man wouldn't let it go. "No, I owe you my life," he repeated.

"Thank you," said Sullenberger with a smile. "That means a lot."

The man sitting next to him was more demonstrative. He gave Sullenberger an awkward hug with one arm. "Thank you, you saved my life," he said. "You're my hero."

"You're welcome," Sullenberger replied.

Rescuers tossed a rope to survivors awaiting help in a raft.

Vince Lombardi

Hudson River, New York
January 15, 2009, 3:38 p.m.

Having gotten everyone off the plane's right wing, Lombardi turned his attention to the raft below. He could see there were two women in the

raft who needed help, and quickly. One looked as old as his grandmother. She was shivering and crying. The younger woman wore a flight attendant's uniform and was bleeding badly from her leg.

Others in the raft and the deckhands above managed to push and pull the injured flight attendant aboard the ferry. But the old woman posed more of a problem. She clearly couldn't climb the ladder, even with help. Lombardi decided there was only one thing to do. He had the deckhands lower lines to the raft. Then he told people on the raft to jury-rig a rope chair. They did so and got the woman into it. The deckhands pulled up the lines and hoisted her to the deck. Ferry passengers quickly moved to assist her, giving her blankets and clothes. Lombardi smiled, shook his head, and watched as more people made their way up the ladder.

Brittany Catanzaro

Hudson River, New York
January 15, 2009, 3:38 p.m.

Twenty-year-old ferry captain Brittany Catanzaro was heading for Manhattan on her boat, *Thomas Kean.* Suddenly she saw the downed plane a short distance away. It looked to her oddly like a child's toy in the bathtub. She wasted no time in following other boats to assist in the rescue effort.

Catanzaro was the youngest ever and first female ferry captain working for New York Waterways. She had been on the water since age 2, sailing on her father's 60-foot pleasure boat. She had also worked as a machinery technician in the Coast Guard.

Within minutes Catanzaro reached the plane's wings. The strong current made holding her position a challenge, but she was able to do it. She counted as 26 survivors climbed aboard the ferry.

Ferry captain Brittany Catanzaro and members of her crew

When the wing was clear of people she turned
the boat around and headed for Manhattan's
Pier 79 at West 39th Street. She smiled as
she saw one passenger hug a deckhand. She
wondered if any of them had noticed the captain
was a woman. She figured that, like her, they had
other things on their minds.

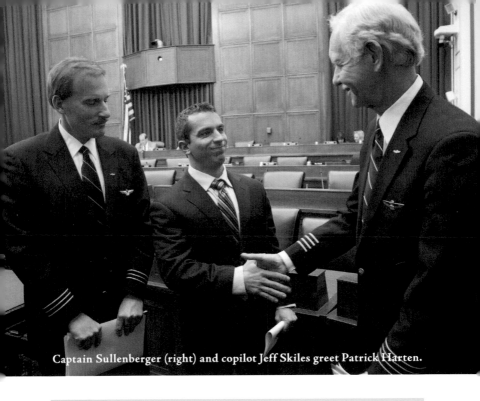

Captain Sullenberger (right) and copilot Jeff Skiles greet Patrick Harten.

Patrick Harten

Westbury, Long Island, New York
January 15, 2009, 3:41 p.m.

Harten sat in the union office, sad and depressed. He was grateful for the union representative there to keep him company, but he didn't feel much like talking. There was no television to watch the news, and he was convinced

Flight 1549 had crashed. Like any air traffic controller who loses a plane, he was immediately relieved of his post. He wouldn't be able to go home until drug testers came. They would take a urine sample and give him a Breathalyzer test. No one suspected he was on drugs or had been drinking on the job. It was just standard procedure in such cases.

He kept thinking about what else he could have done to bring the US Airways Airbus safely to the ground. He wanted to call his wife and tell her what had happened, but he feared he'd lose control of his emotions. He decided to text her instead. "Had a crash," he wrote. "Not OK. Can't talk now."

A few minutes later, a friend put his head in the doorway, a grin on his face. "It looks like they're going to make it," he said. "They're on the wings of the plane."

Harten let out a long sigh of relief. The pilot had made a safe landing after all. Harten felt like a huge weight had been lifted from his shoulders.

Sully Sullenberger

Hudson River, New York
January 15, 2009, 3:44 p.m.

Sullenberger watched as men on the ferries lowered webbed maritime rescue devices to the rafts. Passengers could climb the webbing up to the ferries. He made certain he was the last person to leave the raft before he climbed aboard the *Athena*.

As he reached for the ladder, his fingers felt stiff from the cold. He had to use his forearms to pull himself up the rungs. Once aboard he counted 17 other passengers, including Skiles. Then he remembered his wife at home and pulled his cell phone off his belt.

Lorrie Sullenberger

Danville, California
January 15, 2009, 3:46 p.m.

Lorrie Sullenberger was speaking to a friend when her husband's phone number came up.

Lorrie Sullenberger did not learn of Flight 1549's peril until her husband was safely back on the ground and off of the Hudson River.

She ignored it at first, thinking it couldn't be anything important and she could call him back. But when he continued ringing, she switched over to take his call.

"I wanted to call to say I'm OK," he told her.

"That's good," she replied, rather puzzled.

Why was he calling to tell her that?

"No," he went on, "there's been an incident."

His flight has been delayed from LaGuardia, she thought.

"We hit birds," he continued. "We lost thrust in both engines. I ditched the airplane in the Hudson."

In an instant her heart was in her throat. "Are you OK?" she managed to ask.

"Yes," he said, "but I can't talk now. I'm on my way to the pier. I'll call you from there."

Lorrie Sullenberger hung up the phone and went to the bedroom and lay down. Then she called a friend who advised her, "Go get your girls." She drove to the school her two daughters attended and brought them home to wait for more news.

Joe Hart

Hudson River, New York
January 15, 2009, 3:48 p.m.

While other survivors on the ferryboat *Moira Smith* were thinking about dry clothes and warming up, Hart was thinking about getting home. He called the airline on his cell phone.

"I don't know if you know this," he told the woman who answered, "but my plane went down in the Hudson. . . ."

"Oh my god! Oh my god—are you on it?" she replied.

"I'm fine. I need to know what's the last available flight out of LaGuardia or Newark?"

She told him there was a 6 p.m. and 9:30 p.m. flight out of Newark to Charlotte. After thinking about this for a moment, he realized he'd never make the 6 p.m. flight. Seven other passengers quickly decided they'd join him for the later flight. Their desire to get home apparently overcame their fear of flying, despite the grueling experience they'd just endured.

Sully Sullenberger

Hudson River, New York
January 15, 2009, 3:50 p.m.

After speaking to his wife, Sullenberger decided he should let the airline know about the crash. It seemed likely airline officials had already gotten the news, but he would call just to make sure. He dialed the US Airways Operation Control Center in Pittsburgh, Pennsylvania.

"This is Bob," said a voice Sullenberger recognized as Bob Haney, airline operations manager.

"This is Captain Sullenberger," he replied.

"I can't talk now," said Haney. "There's a plane down in the Hudson!"

"I know," said Sullenberger. "I'm the guy."

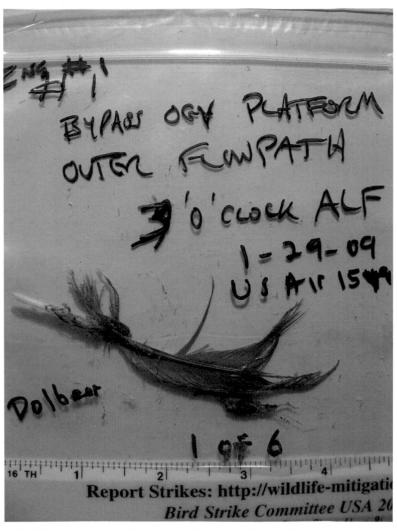

A bird feather recovered from one of the aircraft's heavily damaged engines

First responders rushed to the scene and helped evacuate passengers and crew from the river.

MIRACLE ON THE HUDSON

Sully Sullenberger

Manhattan, New York
January 15, 2009, 3:55 p.m.

Sullenberger followed the other survivors off the *Athena*. On shore at the ferry terminal, he found Captain Don Britt waiting for him. Britt was the US Airways union representative at LaGuardia. He was there to give the pilots moral support and help with any needs they might have.

Sullenberger looked around at the survivors milling in the terminal. Some were drinking cups of steaming coffee or cocoa. Some were hugging each other and giving high fives. Others were trying to stay warm in their wet clothes by standing on a heating grate. Reporters from the media were already gathering as well, eager to get the story of Flight 1549 firsthand from survivors.

New York Governor David Paterson praised Captain Sullenberger and his crew for saving the lives of everyone on their plane.

A police officer approached Sullenberger. He told him New York Mayor Michael Bloomberg and Police Commissioner Raymond Kelly wanted to meet him at another location. Sullenberger politely said he couldn't leave the terminal yet. "I have responsibilities here," he explained. The biggest responsibility for him was making sure all 155 people from the plane were now safe.

Within minutes the mayor, police commissioner, and New York Governor David Paterson all arrived at the terminal. All three congratulated Sullenberger for getting the plane safely down without loss of life. Mayor Bloomberg had aides hand out cell phones to any survivors who needed them to call home. Then he asked Sullenberger for an update on the survivors. "We're trying to find out if they're all accounted for," Sullenberger replied.

Governor Paterson, surrounded by microphones, spoke to the media. "This is a heroic pilot," he said, gesturing to Sullenberger. "We had a *Miracle on 34th Street*," he continued, referring to a popular Christmas movie set in New York City. "I believe now we have had a Miracle on the Hudson."

Lucille Palmer

Manhattan, New York
January 15, 2009, 4:15 p.m.

Palmer didn't know what all the fuss was about. The authorities insisted that she and Diane, along with many other survivors, be taken to St. Luke's–Roosevelt Hospital. Certainly there were people with injuries, including that poor flight attendant with the deep cut in her leg. But she and Diane were not injured.

St. Luke's–Roosevelt Hospital in New York City cared for some of the passengers evacuated from the sinking plane.

At the hospital, the nurse who examined Palmer and her daughter was surprised. All she could find was a small bruise on Palmer from the rope chair that hoisted her up to the ferry. "Were you the ones in the plane crash?" another nurse asked. "Your hair is perfect, your nails are done. Who knew?"

Sully Sullenberger

Manhattan, New York
January 15, 2009, 6:30 p.m.

Sullenberger was getting agitated. He and his crew had agreed to go to the hospital to be checked out. They were found to be in good health but remained in the examination room. They were all waiting for someone to tell them where to go next.

Everyone who came by to check on them heard the same question from Sullenberger: "What's the total?" He couldn't rest until he knew that every passenger had been accounted for. Then a union rep came into the room. He announced that a final count had been tallied and every one of the 155 people aboard Flight 1549 was safe and sound. "It's official," he said.

For the first time since the birds struck his plane, Sully Sullenberger felt at peace.

Carl Bazarian (right) and Brian Wetzel, passengers on Flight 1549, were met by a throng of reporters when they arrived in North Carolina.

Joe Hart

LaGuardia Airport, Queens, New York
January 15, 2009, 11:30 p.m.

The bus ride to LaGuardia had been a bumpy one. The driver got lost on the way, and the eight men began to worry they might miss their late flight. At the airport Hart noticed that all the TVs in a terminal bar were turned to the sports channel ESPN. One in their group, Paul Jorgensen, asked the bartender to turn to the news channel CNN. Jorgensen and the rest wanted to hear the latest reports on the crash.

But the bartender refused. He explained that someone from US Airways had requested that the TVs be changed from CNN. People at the airline didn't want news of Flight 1549 being broadcast in the terminal and causing other passengers to panic.

Hart's group lumbered on to the gate. The plane was leaving on the same runway the men had been on earlier that day on Flight 1549. Hart and the others, in their Red Cross blankets and damp clothes, entered the small plane. They made their way to the rear, drawing stares from the other passengers. Hart sat back nervously as the plane took off, wondering if his companions felt the same. None of them said a word as it rose in the sky. When the plane reached 10,000 feet without any thuds of birds hitting the engines, they all seemed to relax. Someone called out, "It's time for a drink."

Hart thought again about the incredible events of the day. He and the others had survived a potential disaster, thanks to a courageous pilot and his crew. Now they were headed to North Carolina once again. And this time it looked like they'd make it.

EPILOGUE

"The Miracle on the Hudson" became a major news event across the United States. The happy ending to what could have been a terrible tragedy captured the public imagination. Overnight, Sully Sullenberger became a national hero, while the crew and the survivors were thrust into the media spotlight. They gave interviews and appeared on television talk shows and the news program *60 Minutes.* The story of Flight 1549 seemed to give a welcome boost of optimism to many Americans.

The survivors themselves gained something more important—a thankfulness for their lives. Eric Stevenson spoke for many of the survivors when he said, "I don't want to waste this opportunity and I don't want to isolate it. Instead it can help me become a better person." Many survivors informally banded together in what they called the "1549 Club." They have kept in contact with each other on social media since that fateful day in January 2009.

Captain Sullenberger returned to work after his famous water landing and continued to fly until his retirement the following year.

A reunion of Flight 1549 passengers and crew

Captain Sully Sullenberger's life has not been the same since the crash. Not long afterward, he attended a reunion for survivors of Flight 1549 in Charlotte, North Carolina. At the reunion Sullenberger met passengers and their families.

People praised and thanked him. "Thank you for not making me a widow," said the spouse of one survivor. While attending a Broadway play with his family, the show's lead actress singled out Sullenberger at the curtain call.

The audience gave him a 90-second standing ovation. President-elect Barack Obama invited the Sullenbergers to attend his inauguration on January 20, 2009. A movie titled *Sully*, directed by Hollywood legend Clint Eastwood, was

Oscar-winning actor Tom Hanks (left) with Sully Sullenberger. Hanks portrayed Sullenberger in a movie about Flight 1549.

released in 2016. It told the story of Flight 1549, with Tom Hanks playing Sullenberger and Aaron Eckhart cast as copilot Jeff Skiles.

Sullenberger retired from US Airways in March 2010. He served as chairman of the Experimental Aircraft Association's (EAA) Young Eagle program from 2009 to 2013. As chairman, Sullenberger worked to advance the program's goal of fostering interest in aviation for young people. He has written two books about his life experiences and speaks in public about airline safety. A humble man who doesn't consider himself a hero, Sullenberger had this advice for his two daughters in his book *Highest Duty*: "I want them to invest in themselves, to never stop learning, either professionally or personally. At the end of their lives, like all of us, I expect they might ask themselves a simple question: 'Did I make a difference?' My wish for them is that the answer to that question will be yes."

Jeff Skiles joined Sullenberger as cochairman of the EAA's Young Eagle program in 2010.

Two years later he was named vice president of Chapters and Youth Organizations for EAA and retired from US Airways. He eventually left EAA and returned to piloting, working for American Airlines. He has a second career as a motivational speaker for businesses and other organizations.

Doreen Welsh continued to experience the traumatic effects of the crash and her injury. After a year of therapy, she retired from her job at US Airways. She also has taken to the professional speaker podium, calling her set speech "90 Seconds to Impact."

Patrick Harten continues to work as an air traffic controller for LaGuardia Airport. In 2012 he was involved in another disaster. Hurricane Sandy destroyed much of his home in Long Beach Township in New Jersey. Hearing about Harten's troubles, Sullenberger asked his many followers on Twitter to help Harten and others suffering from the hurricane. Harten still occasionally gets text messages from passengers of Flight 1549 when they pass through LaGuardia. "They want me to watch their planes," he says.

Andrew Gray and Stephanie King were married in August 2009 in Wisconsin. Jeff Skiles attended the wedding. Sullenberger couldn't be there, but he sent the couple a four-minute video. In the video he shared stories about his own marriage and wished the couple well.

Eric Stevenson continues to live in Paris. Soon after the crash, John Howell returned to Charlotte. Emma Cowan was inspired to write a song about her experience, a tribute to Sullenberger and his crew, called "Send Another Prayer." She performed it live on CBS-TV's *Early Show* soon after the crash.

Tess Sosa and her husband, along with others from Flight 1549, sued US Airways for not being generous enough in compensating survivors. Each passenger had received a check for $5,000 and a year's upgrade on flights after the disaster. Sosa did not think that was nearly enough. "They are happy they had such amazing results and they applaud themselves, and then give us a small token?" Sosa told reporters. She, her daughter, and other passengers who suffer from

At the Carolinas Aviation Museum in Charlotte, North Carolina, Captain Sullenberger walked through the cabin of the plane he safely landed on the Hudson River. The recovered plane was moved to the museum in 2011 and became a popular attraction.

post-traumatic stress disorder want US Airways' insurance company to pay for therapy. They agreed to pay for a small number of therapy sessions.

Lucille Palmer died on April 2, 2015, at home in Goshen, New York, at age 91. Sullenberger called her "a bright light of life" in a note to her daughter, Diane. Joe Hart is still a sales rep, and Remington Chin is vice president of Audax Group, an investment firm. Brittany Catanzaro still runs her ferry between New Jersey and New York City.

Vince Lombardi played himself in the film *Sully*. In November 2017 he and his crew were involved in another heroic rescue. They saved a man trying to jump into the Hudson River at Battery Park City, Manhattan.

TIMELINE

3:25 P.M.—US Airways Flight 1549 takes off from LaGuardia Airport in New York City for Charlotte, North Carolina.

3:27:11 P.M.—The plane strikes a large flock of birds and loses power in both engines.

3:28:46 P.M.—Flight 1549 glides over the George Washington Bridge.

3:29:11 P.M.—The pilot, Captain Chesley Sullenberger, makes the decision to land the powerless plane on the Hudson River.

3:30:43 P.M.—Sullenberger lands his plane on the river.

3:31 P.M.—Over the next three minutes, 155 crew and passengers evacuate the sinking plane and go into inflatable rafts or onto the plane's wings.

3:34 P.M.—The ferry *Thomas Jefferson* is the first of numerous vessels to reach the plane and start rescuing passengers.

3:44 P.M.—Captain Sullenberger is the last person to leave his raft and climb aboard the ferry *Athena*.

3:54 P.M.—The *Athena* arrives at the Manhattan ferry terminal where survivors are met by emergency crews and police officers.

4:05 P.M.—Sullenberger meets New York Mayor Michael Bloomberg and updates him and New York Governor David Paterson about the crash and the rescue effort.

4:15 P.M.—About 55 survivors, including flight attendant Doreen Welsh, the most seriously injured person, are brought to St. Luke's–Roosevelt Hospital for medical care.

6:30 P.M.—After being examined by doctors at the hospital, Sullenberger receives official word that all 155 people aboard the plane are safe and accounted for.

11:45 P.M.—A group of eight passengers from Flight 1549 takes off in another plane from LaGuardia for Charlotte.

JANUARY 20, 2009—Sullenberger and his wife, Lorrie, are guests of President Barack Obama at his presidential inauguration.

FEBRUARY 2009—Many survivors and their family members have a reunion with the crew of Flight 1549 in Charlotte.

SEPTEMBER 2016—*Sully*, a film about the heroic flight, directed by Clint Eastwood and starring Tom Hanks as Sullenberger, opens.

GLOSSARY

air traffic controller (ar TRAF-ik kuhn-TRO-luhnr)—a worker who helps maintain the safe movement of planes at and between airports

jury-rig (JOOR-e-rig)—to put together quickly from whatever materials are at hand

manifest (MAN-uh-fest)—a list of passengers carried by a plane or other transport vehicle

Mayday (MAY-day)—an international distress call

protocol (PRO-tuh-kol)—regulations and procedures that a government or agency must carry out

terminal (TUR-muhn-l)—a departure and arrival building for passengers at an airport

terrain (tuh-RAYN)—a stretch of land

tourniquet (TUR-ni-kit)—a device to stop bleeding by compressing blood vessels

CRITICAL THINKING QUESTIONS

1. The nation embraced the so-called Miracle on the Hudson as a great event. Why was this so? What part did national and world circumstances play in this response?

2. Captain Sully Sullenberger, the pilot who brought down the plane safely without losing a single life, was hailed as a national hero. However, he didn't see himself as a hero—just a man doing his job. Do you agree? What qualities make a person a hero?

3. Many Flight 1549 survivors say that the disaster and its outcome changed their lives forever. They look at the world in a different way and are grateful to be alive. Do you think this is true for most people who survive near-death experiences? Why or why not?

INTERNET SITES

Use FactHound to find Internet sites related to this book.

Visit *www.facthound.com*

Just type in 9781543541953 and go.

FURTHER READING

Amidon Lusted, Marcia. *Surviving Accidents and Crashes.* Minneapolis, Minn.: Lerner Publishing Group, 2014.

Burgan, Michael. *World War II Pilots: An Interactive History Adventure.* North Mankato, Minn.: Capstone Press, 2013.

Leavitt, Amie Jane. *Anatomy of a Plane Crash.* North Mankato, Minn.: Capstone Press, 2011.

Otfinoski, Steven. *Pilots in Peril!* North Mankato, Minn.: Capstone Young Readers, 2016.

Rodgers, Tamarin. *The Biography of Chesley "Sully" Sullenberger.* North Charleston, S.C.: CreateSpace Independent Publishing Platform, 2017.

Spilsbury, Richard. *Great Aircraft Designs 1900–Today.* Chicago, Ill.: Heinemann-Raintree, 2016.

SELECTED BIBLIOGRAPHY

"Australian songwriter Emma Sophina sings praises of pilot of US Airways Flight 1549." *Daily News*, January 16, 2009.

Dwyer, Jim. "Old Hands on the River Didn't Have to Be Told What to Do." *New York Times*, January 16, 2009.

Hewitt, Bill, and Nicole Weisensee Egan. "Flight 1549: The Right Stuff." *People*, February 23, 2009.

Pilkington, Ed. "Survivors of the Hudson River Plane Crash." *Guardian*, February 4, 2010.

Prochnau, Bill, and Laura Parker. *Miracle on the Hudson: The Survivors of Flight 1549*. New York: Ballantine Books, 2009.

Sullenberger, Captain Chesley "Sully." *Highest Duty: My Search for What Really Matters*. New York: Harper Collins, 2009.

Wilson, Michael, and Russ Buettnerjan. "After Splash, Nerves, Heroics and Comedy." *New York Times*, January 16, 2009.

INDEX

ABOUT THE AUTHOR

Steven Otfinoski has written more than 200 books for young readers. His previous books in the Tangled History series include *Attack on Pearl Harbor* and *Smooth Seas and a Fighting Chance: The Story of the Sinking of* Titanic. Among his many other books for Capstone is the You Choose book *The Sinking of the* Lusitania. Three of his nonfiction books have been named Books for the Teen Age by the New York Public Library. He lives in Connecticut with his wife and dog.